ARTIST TRANSCRIPTIONS
SAXOPHONE

MW00805045

JOHN SOLOS COLTRANE

Transcribed by Carl Coan
Music Editing by Ravi Coltrane
Editorials by Ronny Schiff

Cover photograph courtesy of Alice Coltrane

ISBN 0-7935-2700-7

HAL•LEONARD®
CORPORATION
7777 W. BLUEMOUND RD. P.O. BOX 13819 MILWAUKEE, WI 53213

John Coltrane C O N T E N T S

BIOGRAPHY 4	Lazy Bird 20
NOTATION GUIDE 7	Like Sonny (Simple Like) 56
SUGGESTED ALTERNATE FINGERINGS . . . 8	Locomotion 23
ALTISSIMO FINGERING CHART 9	Lonnie's Lament 127
NOTES ABOUT THE SESSIONS 10	Moment's Notice 28
All Blues 60	Mr. P.C 90
Bessie's Blues 129	My Favorite Things 109
Blue Train (a/k/a Blue Trane) 15	Naima (a/k/a Niema) 53
Central Park West 102	Oleo 33
Countdown 79	Pursuance 139
Cousin Mary 64	'Round Midnight 12
Crescent 132	So What 44
Equinox 104	Some Other Blues 98
Giant Steps 83	Spiral 69
Giant Steps (alternate take) 47	Syeeda's Song Flute 75
Grand Central 40	DISCOGRAPHY 144
Impressions 120	

John Coltrane

John Coltrane, musician and composer, was the most influen-
tial innovator of modern jazz—a genius on the tenor and soprano
saxophones. He was born on September 23, 1926 in Hamlet, North
Carolina. His father, a tailor by trade, was also a musician, his
mother a fine singer, and his grandfather was a minister.

Coltrane began studying E-flat alto horn, clarinet and alto saxophone in high school, and he continued his studies at Granoff
Studios and the Ornstein School of Music when
his family moved to Philadelphia in 1939. He
started on tenor saxophone rather late, at
age eighteen. It was during this time that he
decided to make music his career and
turned professional.

During World War II, Coltrane played
with the U.S. Navy Band in Hawaii. He
then returned to Philadelphia and
began working with various bands,
including the bands of Joe Webb,
Jimmy Heath, Eddie Vinson and then
with Dizzy Gillespie in the early '50s,
with whom he initially played alto.
Later he played with groups front-
ed by Earl Bostic and the powerful
yet subtle player, Johnny Hodges.
He reached his first major musi-
cal milestone when he joined the Miles Davis Quartet in 1955.
Throughout the year and a half he played with Miles, he continually worked on developing his style, describing it as "...starting in
the middle of a musical sentence and moving in both directions at
once." The result was a confluence of arpeggios spiraling out from
the line—a style dubbed "sheets of sound."

The next move for Coltrane was to Thelonious Monk's group in
1957. With Monk there were wholly original harmonic structures and
unique time patterns. He played more extended solos, and they

were thematically rather than harmonically organized. His range on the instrument grew markedly. Coltrane then went out on his own beyond bebop and into new realms, including discovering the totally different modal (rather than chordal) and rhythmic organization of Indian music. An example of this is his playing on Miles Davis' album *Kind of Blue*.

Two classic albums marked 1959, *Giant Steps* and *Coltrane Jazz*, with the contrasting tunes of "Naima," "Mr. P.C." and "Giant Steps" soon to become jazz standards. Later, Coltrane's use of soprano sax on the album *My Favorite Things* brought that instrument into the mainstream of jazz.

In 1960, Coltrane formed his famous quartet consisting of McCoy Tyner on piano, Elvin Jones on drums and Jimmy Garrison on bass, and they began creating some of the most unique and expressive music in jazz history. Quoting from Leonard Feather, "This innovation of Indian and modal ideas led to greater freedom for jazz soloists in the '60s, taking the music away from improvisations on songs or song patterns and allowing it to move toward a wholly new musical feeling."

Yet the music Coltrane recorded in the early '60s covered a wide range of styles—blues, ballads, standards and Indian. Full recognition of his talents came in 1961, when he won the *downbeat* Critics' Polls for "Tenor Sax," "Miscellaneous Instrument" (soprano sax) and "New Star Combo." He continued to win at least one *downbeat* award a year from thereon. He was consistently lauded for his sensitivity and intensity, for his ability to change and experiment, and for his absolute mastery of his instrument.

Critics acclaimed many albums such as *Lush Life, Giant Steps, Live At The Village Vanguard, Africa Brass, My Favorite Things, Impressions, Black Pearls, Transition,* and *Meditations.* However, it was the profoundly spiritual four-movement suite, *A Love Supreme,* that received the most accolades, including *downbeat*'s "Record of the Year." That same year, 1965, Coltrane simultaneously received *downbeat*'s "Hall of Fame," "Jazzman of the Year" and "Tenor Sax" awards in the *Readers' Poll.*

Coltrane embraced the concept of free jazz, but sought unifying elements for it within his own group. However in '65, Coltrane began to experiment and augment his quartet, seeking a freer and denser sound. Over the course of time, he was joined by various talents that included Pharoah Sanders (their collaboration produced the album, *Meditations*), Archie Shepp, Freddie Hubbard and Rashied Ali. Tyner and Jones left the group to be replaced by Alice McLeod [Coltrane] (of whom Coltrane said, "...she continually senses the right colors, the right textures of the sound of the chords.") and the looser, mobile Ali on drums. These changes ushered in yet another experimental phase in the Coltrane sound.

John Coltrane died on July 17, 1967 at age 40, leaving a wealth of his ingenious music. The music Coltrane created is deeply spiritual and emotional and evokes a similar response in those who appreciate its significance. Coltrane felt we must all make a conscious effort to effect positive change in the world and that his music was an instrument to create positive thought patterns in the minds of the people. He had a continual quest for growth and expansion of his music. He said on the liner notes of *Live At The Village Vanguard,* "I've really got to work and study more approaches to writing. I've already been looking into those approaches to music, as in India, in which particular sounds and scales are intended to produce specific emotional meanings. I've got to keep probing. There's so much more to do."

"In 'Giant Steps,' I feel like I can't hear but so much in the ordinary chords we usually have going in the accompaniment," Coltrane said. "I just have to have more of a blueprint. It may be that sometimes I've been trying to force all those extra progressions into a structure...I have [a] whole lot of things I'm working on, sometimes I find that I am playing them all at once."

His philosophy and musical dedication led him to encourage and influence many musicians—a legacy that remains as strong today as it was in the past. His influence on jazz and contemporary music has been critically acclaimed throughout the world.

He remains a legend, a man of mystique who set no perimeters around his creative genius, a man often recognized as being ahead of his time.

Ronny Schiff

* excerpts were taken from the *First* and *Second Annual Coltrane Festival* programs, courtesy of Alice Coltrane

Notation Guide

+   ·   Alternate Fingering (see chart)

✗   ·   Ghost Note

L.D.   ·   Lip Down from previous note

H.T.   ·   Half Tongue

(b) (#)   ·   Note is slightly sharp or flat

⌐⌐   ·   Bend note using jaw

⊕   ·   Special Alternate Fingering (see chart)

8vA ↓   ·   Play note up an octave

F↓   ·   Finger 8vb, sounds as written

F↑   ·   Finger 8va, sounds as written

L.D.'   ·   Finger note 1/2 step higher and lip down (actual pitch is given)

SUGGESTED ALTERNATE FINGERINGS*

T. = OCTAVE KEY   ⊗ = FRONT F KEY   ⊕ = SPECIAL ALTERNATE FINGERING

*Suggested by Carl Coan

ALTISSIMO FINGERING CHART*

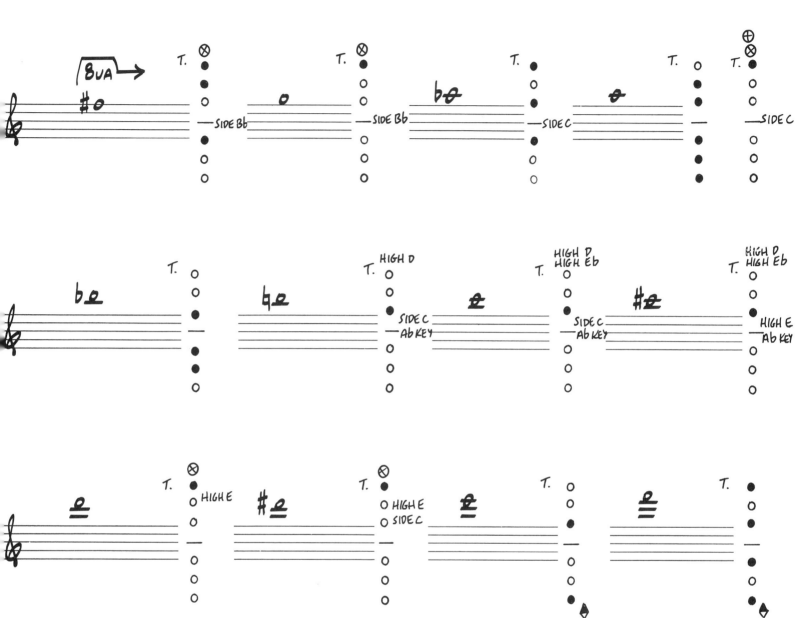

Notes about the sessions...

What follows is a list of the sessions plus the date and place of recording. The personnel listed are those Coltrane employed for his own sessions or with whom Coltrane played with on other leaders' recordings. Much of this information was gleaned by Michael Cuscuna from the files of Columbia, Atlantic and Blue Note Records and David Wild from the ABC-Impulse files. Often, alternate takes from these sessions were kept in the can and put on other recordings. Not only were many of these sessions milestones (no pun intended) in the jazz world, but the list of sidemen reads like a "Who's Who" of consummate jazzmen of mid-20th century. There are instances, such as the Miles Davis recordings, where the recording venue information was not available.

(*Note*: In the age of single track recording, notice how quickly some of the sessions were done, such as the *Giant Step* sessions that occurred on May 4th and May 5th, 1959. Not only were the six album cuts done, but also three alternate takes that can be found on other albums [see the album *Alternate Takes*] and two unissued cuts.)

'ROUND MIDNIGHT—The classic Thelonious Monk composition recorded with the Miles Davis Quintet on September 10, 1956 in New York City, including Davis on trumpet, Coltrane on tenor, Red Garland on piano, "Philly Joe" Jones on drums. (Coltrane played with Monk's group the following year.)

BLUE TRAIN (a/k/a **BLUE TRANE**)—Recorded at Van Gelder Studios, Hackensack, New Jersey, September 15, 1957, by the John Coltrane Sextet: Coltrane on tenor, Lee Morgan trumpet, Curtis Fuller on trombone, Kenny Drew on piano, Paul Chambers on bass, "Philly Joe" Jones on drums.

LAZY BIRD—Recorded at Van Gelder Studios, Hackensack, New Jersey, September 15, 1957, by the John Coltrane Sextet: Coltrane on tenor, Lee Morgan trumpet, Curtis Fuller on trombone, Kenny Drew on piano, Paul Chambers on bass, "Philly Joe" Jones on drums.

LOCOMOTION—Recorded at Van Gelder Studios, Hackensack, New Jersey, September 15, 1957, by the John Coltrane Sextet: Coltrane on tenor, Lee Morgan trumpet, Curtis Fuller on trombone, Kenny Drew on piano, Paul Chambers on bass, "Philly Joe" Jones on drums.

MOMENT'S NOTICE—Recorded at Van Gelder Studios, Hackensack, New Jersey, September 15, 1957, by the John Coltrane Sextet: Coltrane on tenor, Lee Morgan trumpet, Curtis Fuller on trombone, Kenny Drew on piano, Paul Chambers on bass, "Philly Joe" Jones on drums.

OLEO—Sonny Rollins' composition recorded at the Plaza Hotel by the Miles Davis Sextet in New York City, September 9, 1958 with Davis on trumpet, Cannonball Adderley on alto sax, Coltrane on tenor, Bill Evans on piano, Paul Chambers on bass, Jimmy Cobb on drums.

GRAND CENTRAL—Recorded with the Cannonball Adderley Quintet at Universal Studios in Chicago, February 3, 1959 with Adderley on alto sax, Coltrane on tenor, Wynton Kelly on piano, Paul Chambers on bass, Jimmy Cobb on drums.

SO WHAT—A Miles Davis composition recorded March 2, 1959 in New York City with the Miles Davis Sextet including Davis on trumpet, Cannonball Adderley on alto sax, Coltrane on tenor, Bill Evans on piano, Paul Chambers on bass, Jimmy Cobb on drums.

GIANT STEPS (alternate take), **NAIMA,** (a/k/a **NIEMA**), **LIKE SONNY (SIMPLE LIKE)**—Recorded in New York City, April 1, 1959 by the John Coltrane Quartet: Coltrane on tenor, Cedar Walton on piano, Paul Chambers on bass, Lex Humphries on drums.

ALL BLUES—A Miles Davis composition recorded April 22, 1959 in New York with the Miles Davis Sextet including Davis on trumpet, Cannonball Adderley on alto sax, Coltrane on tenor, Bill Evans on piano, Paul Chambers on bass, Jimmy Cobb on drums.

COUSIN MARY, SPIRAL—Recorded in New York City at the Atlantic Recording Studios, May 4, 1959 by the John Coltrane Quartet: Coltrane on tenor, Tommy Flanagan on piano, Paul Chambers on bass, Art Taylor on drums.

SYEEDA'S SONG FLUTE, COUNTDOWN, GIANT STEPS, MR. P.C.—A continuation of the May 4th session on May 5, 1959 with the same personnel. All of the above songs on the landmark recording *Giant Steps*.

SOME OTHER BLUES—Recorded at the Atlantic Recording Studios, New York City, November 24, 1959 with Coltrane on tenor, Wynton Kelly on piano, Paul Chambers on bass, Jimmy Cobb on drums.

CENTRAL PARK WEST—Recorded in New York City at the Atlantic Recording Studios, October 24, 1960 by the John Coltrane Quartet: Coltrane on tenor, McCoy Tyner on piano, Steve Davis on bass, Elvin Jones on drums.

EQUINOX—Recorded in New York City at the Atlantic Recording Studios, October 26, 1960 by the John Coltrane Quartet: Coltrane on tenor, McCoy Tyner on piano, Steve Davis on bass, Elvin Jones on drums.

MY FAVORITE THINGS—Rodgers and Hammerstein's composition; many recordings by Coltrane. This cut recorded in New York City at the Atlantic Recording Studios, October 21, 1960 by the John Coltrane Quartet: Coltrane on tenor and soprano saxes, McCoy Tyner on piano, Steve Davis on bass, Elvin Jones on drums.

IMPRESSIONS—Recorded on tour at Koncerthuset, Stockholm, Sweden, November 23, 1961 (originally a private tape) by the John Coltrane Quintet: Coltrane on tenor and soprano saxes, Eric Dolphy on alto sax, bass clarinet and flute, McCoy Tyner on piano, Reggie Workman on bass, Elvin Jones on drums.

LONNIE'S LAMENT—Recorded at Van Gelder Studios, Englewood, New Jersey, April 27th, 1964 by the John Coltrane Quartet: Coltrane on tenor, McCoy Tyner on piano, Jimmy Garrison on bass, Elvin Jones on drums.

BESSIE'S BLUES, CRESCENT—Recorded at Van Gelder Studios, Englewood, New Jersey, June 1, 1964 by the John Coltrane Quartet: Coltrane on tenor, McCoy Tyner on piano, Jimmy Garrison on bass, Elvin Jones on drums (apparently had been recorded earlier, on April 27th, and these takes were not used and have been lost).

PURSUANCE (from *A LOVE SUPREME*)—Recorded at Van Gelder Studios, Englewood, New Jersey, December 10, 1964 by John Coltrane Sextet: Coltrane and Archie Shepp on tenor saxes, McCoy Tyner on piano, Jimmy Garrison and Art Davis on basses, Elvin Jones on drums. The recording that received the most accolades for Coltrane.

'ROUND MIDNIGHT

Words by BERNIE HANIGHEN
Music by COOTIE WILLIAMS and THELONIOUS MONK

BLUE TRAIN
(a/k/a BLUE TRANE)

By JOHN COLTRANE

LAZY BIRD

By JOHN COLTRANE

LOCOMOTION

By JOHN COLTRANE

(TENOR)

STRAIGHT AHEAD (♩ = 276)

MOMENT'S NOTICE

By JOHN COLTRANE

OLEO

By SONNY ROLLINS

*1 FINGERED AS Eb, OVERTONE SOUNDS AS Bb.
*2 FINGERED AS D, OVERTONE SOUNDS AS A

GRAND CENTRAL

By JOHN COLTRANE

SO WHAT

By Miles Davis

GIANT STEPS

By JOHN COLTRANE

✴ FINGER AS E, OVERTONE SOUNDS AS B

NAIMA
(a/k/a NIEMA)

By JOHN COLTRANE

LIKE SONNY
(SIMPLE LIKE)

By JOHN COLTRANE

FOR HEAD ONLY: HIGH Bb ⊕ = T.   HIGH E ⊕ = T.

All Blues

By MILES DAVIS

COUSIN MARY

By JOHN COLTRANE

SPIRAL

By JOHN COLTRANE

* FINGERED AS Eb, OVERTONE SOUNDS AS Bb

SYEEDA'S SONG FLUTE

By JOHN COLTRANE

COUNTDOWN

By JOHN COLTRANE

* FINGERED AS D, OVERTONE SOUNDS AS A

GIANT STEPS

By JOHN COLTRANE

* FINGERED AS D, OVERTONE SOUNDS AS A

MR. P.C.

By JOHN COLTRANE

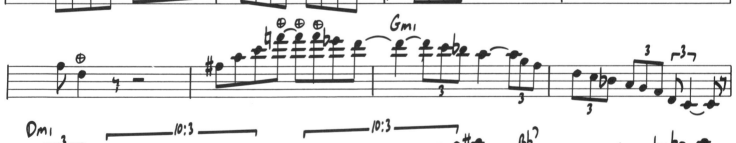

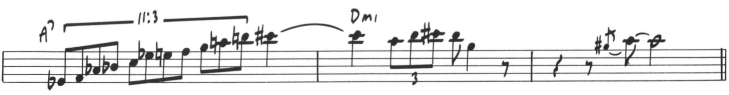

SOME OTHER BLUES

By JOHN COLTRANE

*DURING THE SOLO THE BAND IS PLAYING STANDARD BLUES CHANGES.

FOURS = 4 BARS OF TENOR, 4 BARS OF DRUMS
*HIGH F# = PLAY USING FRONT F KEY, 2 AND SIDE Bb —
NO 1 IN RT. HAND AS IN REGULAR HIGH F#

CENTRAL PARK WEST

By JOHN COLTRANE

EQUINOX

By JOHN COLTRANE

MY FAVORITE THINGS
from THE SOUND OF MUSIC

Lyrics by OSCAR HAMMERSTEIN II
Music by RICHARD RODGERS

* SIDE "D"

IMPRESSIONS

By JOHN COLTRANE

LONNIE'S LAMENT

By JOHN COLTRANE

BESSIE'S BLUES

By JOHN COLTRANE

131

CRESCENT

By JOHN COLTRANE

(TENOR)

PURSUANCE
Part III of A LOVE SUPREME

By JOHN COLTRANE

Discography

Title	Album	Cat. No.	Date
'Round Midnight	'Round About Midnight (Miles Davis)	Columbia 40610	9/56
Blue Train	Blue Train	Blue Note BST 81577	9/57
Lazy Bird	Blue Train	Blue Note BST 81577	9/57
Locomotion	Blue Train	Blue Note BST 81577	9/57
Moment's Notice	Blue Train	Blue Note BST 81577	9/57
Oleo	Jazz At The Plaza (Miles Davis)	Columbia 32470	9/58
Grand Central	Cannonball Adderley Quintet in Chicago	Mercury MG 20499	2/59
So What	Kind Of Blue (Miles Davis)	CBS 40579	3/59
All Blues	Kind Of Blue (Miles Davis)	CBS 40579	4/59
Giant Steps	Alternate Takes	Atlanta 1668	4/59
Like Sonny	Alternate Takes	Atlantic 1668	4/59
Naima	Alternate Takes	Atlantic 1668	4/59
Countdown	Giant Steps	Atlantic SD 1311	5/59
Cousin Mary	Giant Steps	Atlantic SD 1311	5/59
Giant Steps	Giant Steps	Atlantic SD 1311	5/59
Mr. P.C.	Giant Steps	Atlantic SD 1311	5/59
Spiral	Giant Steps	Atlantic SD 1311	5/59
Syeeda's Song Flute	Giant Steps	Atlantic SD 1311	5/59
Some Other Blues	Coltrane Jazz	Atlantic CS 1354	11/59
Central Park West	Best Of John Coltrane	Atlantic SD 1541	10/60
Equinox	Best Of John Coltrane	Atlantic SD 1541	10/60
My Favorite Things	Best Of John Coltrane	Atlantic SD 1541	10/60
Impressions	Coltranology - Volume One	Affinity 32-2051	11/61
Lonnie's Lament	Crescent	Impulse AS-66	4/64
Bessie's Blues	Crescent	Impulse AS-66	6/64
Crescent	Crescent	Impulse AS-66	6/64
Pursuance	A Love Supreme	Impulse AS-9161	12/64